This Journal Belongs To

_____

ROCK
POINT
WWW.ROCKPOINTPUB.COM
NEW YORK, NY

One of the most iconic literary figures in the world, Edgar Allan Poe (1809–1849) was an author and poet who not only helped shape and define the genre of American macabre, but was one of the first American writers to become a major figure in international literature. Poe is considered a pioneer of literary horror with classics such as "The Tell-Tale Heart," "Fall of the House of Usher," and "The Raven." He was also an inspiration to favorite authors including H.P. Lovecraft, Jules Verne, Charles Baudelaire, and Stephen King.

Although his name has become synonymous with horrific frights, premature burial, ancient crypts, and vengeful black cats, Poe was a major contributor to science fiction and an early practitioner of the craft of the short story. A master storyteller, Poe is also known as the inventor of detective fiction who paved the way for characters like Sherlock Holmes and Hercule Poirot.

Poe's effect on pop culture and the public permeates beyond his poetry, fiction, and essays. Examples of Poe's influence have appeared in a broad spectrum of mediums including film, comics, books, theatre, radio, and television. From a film based on the "The Raven" starring actor John Cusak as Poe himself, to an Italian comic book featuring a Poe protagonist with the code name "Raven," the influence of Edgar Allen Poe continues to grow and nurture yet another generation.

Edgar Allan Poe's own life was not any less intriguing than his work. To this day, his death remains a mystery. The cause of his death is unknown, but speculation has included delirium tremens, rabies, syphilis, and cholera. Regardless, his legacy is one that changed the world.

"The thousand injuries of Fortunato I had borne as I best could, but when he ventured upon insult I vowed revenge."

*"The Cask of Amontillado," 1846*

*"A poem deserves its title only inasmuch as it excites, by elevating the soul."*

*"The Poetic Principle,"* 1850

"There neither exists nor can exist any work more thoroughly dignified — more supremely noble than this very poem — this poem per se — this poem which is a poem and nothing more — this poem written solely for the poem's sake."

"The Poetic Principle," 1850

*"Literature is the most noble of professions. In fact, it is about the only one fit for a man. For my own part, there is no seducing me from the path."*

Letter to Frederick W. Thomas, 1849

"With me poetry has been not a purpose, but a passion;
and the passions should be held in reverence."

Preface, *The Raven and Other Poems, 1845*

"Were I called on to define, very briefly, the term 'Art' I should call it 'the reproduction of what the Senses perceive in Nature through the veil of the soul.' The mere imitation, however accurate, of what is in Nature, entitles no man to the sacred name of 'Artist.' "

*"Marginalia," 1844*

*"My life has been whim —impulse —passion —a longing for solitude —a scorn of all things present, in an earnest desire for the future."*

*Letter to James Russell Lowell, 1844*

*"It is impossible that any deed could have been wrought with more thorough deliberation. For weeks—for months—I pondered upon the means of the murder.*

*"The Imp of the Perverse," 1845*

Edgar Allan Poe is widely acknowledged as the inventor of the modern detective story, whose intelligent but eccentric detective Dupin is the predecessor of Arthur Conan Doyle's Sherlock Holmes and Agatha Christie's Hercule Poirot.

"How many good books suffer neglect through the inefficiency of their beginnings!"

"Marginalia," 1844

"In reading some books we occupy ourselves chiefly with the thoughts of the author; in perusing others, exclusively with our own."

*"Marginalia," 1844*

"They who dream by day are cognizant of many things which escape those who dream only by night."

*"Eleonora," 1842*

"I think it was his eye! yes, it was this! One of his eyes resembled that of a vulture —a pale blue eye, with a film over it. Whenever it fell upon me, my blood ran cold; and so by degrees—very gradually—I made up my mind to take the life of the old man, and thus rid myself of the eye for ever."

"The Tell-Tale Heart," 1843

" 'Villains!' I shrieked, 'dissemble no more! I admit the deed! — tear up the planks! — here, here! — it is the beating of his hideous heart!' "

*"The Tell-Tale Heart," 1843*

"I was a child and she was a child,
In this kingdom by the sea,
But we loved with a love that was more than love —
I and my Annabel Lee —
With a love that the wingèd seraphs of Heaven
Coveted her and me."

*"Annabel Lee," 1849*

*"All that we see or seem is but a dream within a dream."*

*"A Dream within a Dream,"* 1849

"He had come like a thief in the night. And one by one dropped the revellers in the blood-bedewed halls of their revel, and died each in the despairing posture of his fall."

*"The Mask of the Red Death,"* 1842

*"I became insane, with long intervals of horrible sanity."*

Letter to George W. Eveleth, 1848

Despite a less than loving relationship between human and feline in his short story "The Black Cat," Poe loved animals, and at the time of his death owned a tortoiseshell named Caterina.

*"I live continually in a reverie of the future."*

*Letter to James Russell Lowell, 1844*

*"The boundaries which divide Life from Death are at best shadowy and vague. Who shall say where the one ends, and where the other begins?"*

"The Premature Burial," 1844

"And the life of the ebony clock went out with that of the last of the gay. And the flames of the tripods expired. And Darkness and Decay and the Red Death held illimitable dominion over all."

*"The Mask of the Red Death," 1842*

*"The true genius shudders at incompleteness - and usually prefers silence to saying something which is not everything it should be."*

*"Marginalia,"* 1848

"*Literature is the most noble of professions. In fact, it is about the only one fit for a man. For my own part, there is no seducing me from the path.*"

*Letter to Frederick W. Thomas, 1849*

*"Ye who read are still among the living, but I who write shall have long since gone my way into the region of shadows."*

*"Shadow—a Parable," 1850*

"Men have called me mad; but the question is not yet settled, whether madness is or is not the loftiest intelligence."

"Eleonora," 1842

"And then there stole into my fancy, like a rich musical note, the thought of what sweet rest there must be in the grave."

*"The Pit and the Pendulum," 1842*

"I felt creeping upon me, by slow yet certain degrees, the wild influences of his own fantastic yet impressive superstitions."

*"The Fall of the House of Usher," 1839*

"We have put her living in the tomb! Said I not that my senses were acute? I now tell you that I heard her first feeble movements in the hollow coffin. I heard them — many, many days ago — yet I dared not — I dared not speak!"

*"The Fall of the House of Usher,"* 1839

"His plans were bold and fiery, and his conceptions glowed with barbaric lustre. There are some who would have thought him mad."

*"The Mask of the Red Death," 1842*

A division of Quarto Publishing Group USA Inc.
276 Fifth Avenue, Suite 206
New York, New York 10001

ROCK POINT and the distinctive Rock Point logo are trademarks of
Quarto Publishing Group USA Inc.

© 2015 by Rock Point

Design by Heidi North
Illustrations © Shutterstock and iStock

ISBN-13: 978-1-93799-457-0

Printed in China

2 4 6 8 10 9 7 5 3 1